CHECKERBOARD BIOGRAPHY LIBRARY

EXPLORERS

Christopher
Columbus

Kristin Petrie

ABDO
Publishing Company

visit us at
www.abdopub.com

Published by ABDO Publishing Company, 4940 Viking Drive, Edina, Minnesota 55435.
Copyright © 2004 by Abdo Consulting Group, Inc. International copyrights reserved in all
countries. No part of this book may be reproduced in any form without written permission from
the publisher.

Printed in the United States.

Cover Photos: Corbis, North Wind
Interior Photos: Corbis pp. 5, 7, 9, 14, 15, 17, 20, 21, 23, 25, 27, 29; North Wind pp. 8, 11, 13

Series Coordinator: Stephanie Hedlund
Editors: Kate A. Conley, Kristin Van Cleaf
Art Direction & Cover Design: Neil Klinepier
Interior Design & Maps: Dave Bullen

Library of Congress Cataloging-in-Publication Data

Petrie, Kristin, 1970-
    Christopher Columbus / Kristin Petrie.
       p. cm. -- (Explorers)
    Includes index.
    Summary: Introduces the life of explorer Christopher Columbus, the first man known to cross
the Atlantic Ocean, and discusses what he found when he reached the islands now known as
the West Indies.
    ISBN 1-59197-595-6
    1. Columbus, Christopher--Juvenile literature. 2. Explorers--America--Biography--Juvenile
literature. 3. Explorers--Spain--Biography--Juvenile literature. 4. America--Discovery and
exploration--Spanish--Juvenile literature. [1. Columbus, Christopher. 2. Explorers. 3. America--
Discovery and exploration--Spanish.] I. Title.

E111.P47 2004
970.01'5'092--dc22
[B]   2003062928

Contents

Christopher Columbus 4

Early Years 6

Before Exploring 8

The Plan 12

The First Voyage 14

Founding Isabella 20

A Third Voyage 22

The High Voyage 26

Final Days 28

Glossary 30

Saying It 31

Web Sites 31

Index 32

Christopher Columbus

In the 1400s, Asian gold, spices, and other valuables were important to Europe. **Caravans** transported these trade items from the East through the vast deserts. Once they reached the Mediterranean Sea, the goods were brought by ship to Europe.

But at that time, Europe was struggling against the Ottoman Empire. It ruled much of the trade route. This fighting made it difficult and **dangerous** to continue trading. In addition, the length of the trip made the goods expensive. So, trading between Europe and the East nearly stopped.

The need for a new route to Asia began an **era** of exploration. This is the world into which Christopher Columbus was born. What do you know about Columbus?

1451
Christopher Columbus born

1485
Hernán Cortés born

1450
John Cabot born

1460
Vasco da Gama born

1491
Jacques Cartier born

Columbus navigated **uncharted** seas and led important expeditions to foreign lands. He was determined to find a western sea route to the mysterious land of Asia. He never reached this goal. However, he did accomplish many things on his search.

Christopher Columbus did not have a portrait painted during his lifetime. But, there are several versions of what people think he looked like.

1492
Columbus's first voyage west for Spain

1496
Cabot's first voyage for England

1493
Columbus's second voyage, attempted to colonize Hispaniola

Early Years

Domenico Colombo and Suzanna Fontanarossa lived in Genoa, Italy. Domenico was a wool weaver. Suzanna's family was also in this trade. The couple owned a weaving shop in Genoa. Domenico also worked as a **gatekeeper** and wine merchant to increase his income.

In 1451, Domenico and Suzanna had the first of their five children. They named him Cristoforo Colombo. We know him as Christopher Columbus.

Christopher and his brothers may have been schooled in a nearby monastery. They learned math, drawing, and Latin. However, they did not learn to read or write. Christopher finished his early education by the time he turned 14.

Outside of school, Christopher helped in his father's shop. It wasn't long before Domenico realized his son was not a weaver.

1497
Cabot's second voyage, discovered the Grand Banks; da Gama was first to sail around Africa to India

1496 or 1497
Hernando de Soto born

1498
Cabot's third voyage, may have died; Columbus's third voyage

When Christopher turned 15, he began to sail on the Mediterranean Sea with local merchants. He traded goods for wealthy families in Genoa. In the 1470s, Christopher took part in his first documented voyage. He was part of a trading expedition to Chios, an island near Turkey.

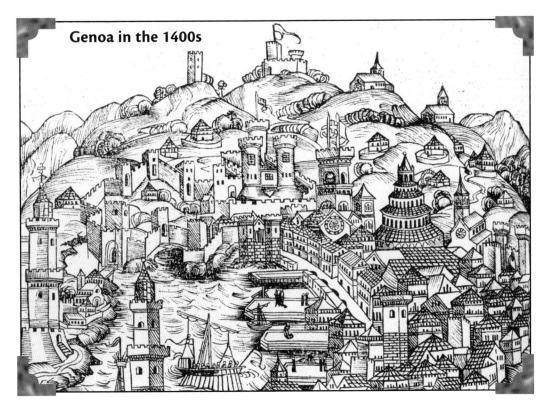

Genoa in the 1400s

1502
Columbus's fourth voyage; da Gama's second voyage

1506
Columbus died

1504
Cortés sailed to the West Indies

Before Exploring

In 1476, Christopher sailed on the Atlantic Ocean for the first time. The ship was headed for the British Isles. According to legend, pirates attacked the ship. Christopher managed to escape and swim a long distance to the shore of Portugal.

An exhausted Christopher made his way to Lisbon. His brother, Bartholomew, lived there. Christopher joined his brother in drawing and selling maps for a while. During this time, Christopher continued to study the sea and dream of what lay beyond the Atlantic Ocean.

Portugal was a great place to be in that **era**. The Portuguese were leading the way

A caravel

1511
Cortés helped take over Cuba

1510
Francisco Vásquez de Coronado born

1514
De Soto went to the New World

in the world of exploration. They had invented the **caravel**.

The caravel was the first type of vessel strong enough to sail against the wind. Christopher would later benefit from the invention of these ships. They would help him cross the Atlantic Ocean.

**Christopher Columbus
as a young man**

**Would
You?**

Would you be able to survive in the world if you only knew some math and drawing? What do you think Columbus should have learned before he started sailing?

While in Lisbon, Christopher met a young woman. Her name was Felipa Perestrello e Moniz. Felipa was the daughter of the governor of Porto Santo. Porto Santo is an island near the northern coast of Africa.

Christopher and Felipa married in 1478. The couple moved to Porto Santo and then to a nearby island called Madeira. In 1480, Felipa and Christopher had a son named Diego. Sadly, Felipa died a few years later. Christopher and Diego then sailed back to Lisbon.

While in Portugal this time, Christopher learned to read and write in Spanish. He learned navigation and **hydrography**, too. This helped Christopher develop his plan to sail west.

Several years later, Christopher and a woman named Beatriz Enríquez de Arana had a son. Christopher's second son, Fernando, was born in 1488.

1524
Da Gama's third voyage, died in Cochin, India

1519–1521
Cortés conquered the Aztec Empire and claimed Mexico for Spain

1532
De Soto helped attack the Inca Empire

Would you want to go back to sea if you had faced pirates?

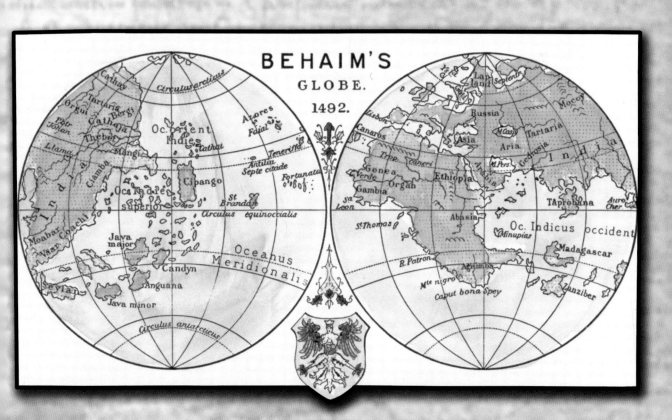

In 1492, North and South America had not yet been discovered. So, they were not included on maps of the world.

The Plan

In the 1400s, the Portuguese were still trying to reach Asia by sailing around Africa. Columbus believed it would be easier to get there by sailing west. During his years of sailing and studying, he had developed a plan. He called it the Enterprise of the Indies.

Columbus's plan was based on a few mistaken ideas. First, he believed the world was much smaller than it is. Second, he believed the world was covered mostly by land, rather than water. With this in mind, Columbus concluded that Asia extended much farther than it does.

Finally, Columbus thought Asia lay just on the other side of the Atlantic Ocean. Europeans didn't yet know that North and South America existed. Columbus planned to sail west along the latitude of the Canary Islands until he reached Japan.

His plan set, Columbus needed money for ships and supplies. In Portugal, King John II turned him down. So,

1534
Cartier's first voyage for France

1539–1542
De Soto explored La Florida

1533
De Soto helped take over Cuzco

1535
Cartier's second voyage

Columbus went to Spain. There, King Ferdinand and Queen Isabella also turned him down. But after six years of repeated proposals, the royals of Spain decided to risk the venture.

Columbus presented his plan to the Spanish royals and their court many times.

Would You?

Would you keep asking for money for six years? How would you present your proposal for a trip like Columbus wanted?

The First Voyage

On August 3, 1492, Columbus started out on his first expedition. He and about 90 crew members left from the small town of Palos, Spain.

Three ships had been provided by families from Palos. The *Pinta* and the *Niña* were **caravels**. Columbus commanded the third and largest ship, the *Santa María*.

Replicas of the *Santa María* (front), *Pinta*, and *Niña*

On August 16, the **fleet** briefly stopped at the Canary Islands. On September 6, it headed west for one month. At this point, Columbus changed his course to the southwest. The sailors began to worry because they had gone so long without seeing land. They started to **rebel** against their captain.

Columbus and his crew sailed in open water for more than a month.
Columbus offered a reward to the first man to sight land. Land was finally
sighted in October 1492. Columbus later claimed the reward for himself.

1547
Cortés died

1557
Cartier died

1542
Coronado returned to New Spain; de Soto died

1554
Coronado died

1566
Drake's first voyage to the New World

To everyone's relief, land was sighted on October 12. The ships landed on an island in the Bahamas. We know it as San Salvador.

Columbus thought he had arrived on an island in the East Indies, near Japan or China. For this reason, he called the islanders *Indians*. Columbus claimed the island for Spain.

Columbus and his crew continued to explore. On October 28, sailors spotted Cuba. Columbus believed they were nearing the mainland of Asia at this point. The **fleet** explored harbor after harbor, looking for Asian cities.

In early December, the expedition reached the northern coast of Hispaniola. Columbus called it *La Isla Española*, which means "the Spanish Island." Today, the island is home to the countries Haiti and the Dominican Republic.

On Christmas Day of 1492, the *Santa María* was shipwrecked on Hispaniola. Columbus left some of his crew on the island to form a colony. He then boarded the *Niña* and rushed back to Spain.

1567
Drake's second voyage

1577
Drake began a worldwide voyage, was first Englishman to sail the Pacific Ocean

1570 and 1572
Drake terrorized the Spanish in the New World

The Spanish royals named Columbus "Admiral of the Ocean Sea." He also became **viceroy** and governor of the land he had discovered.

Columbus claiming his discoveries for Spain

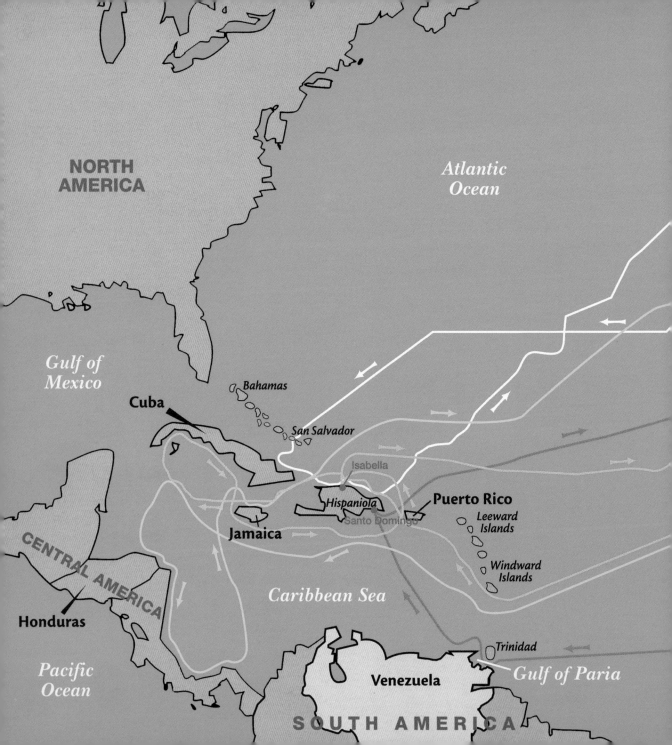

NORTH
AMERICA

*Atlantic
Ocean*

*Gulf of
Mexico*

Bahamas

Cuba

San Salvador

Isabella

Hispaniola

Puerto Rico

*Leeward
Islands*

Santo Domingo

Jamaica

CENTRAL AMERICA

*Windward
Islands*

Honduras

Caribbean Sea

*Pacific
Ocean*

Trinidad

Gulf of Paria

Venezuela

SOUTH AMERICA

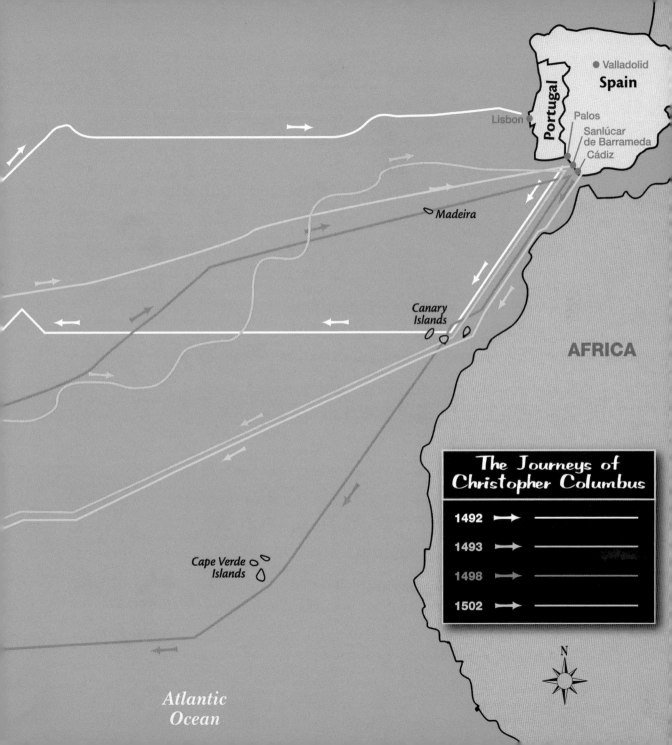

Valladolid

Spain

Portugal

Lisbon

Palos
Sanlúcar
de Barrameda
Cádiz

Madeira

*Canary
Islands*

AFRICA

The Journeys of
Christopher Columbus

1492 ➡ _____
1493 ➡ _____
1498 ➡ _____
1502 ➡ _____

Cape Verde ○ ○
Islands ○

*Atlantic
Ocean*

N

Founding Isabella

In 1493, Ferdinand and Isabella asked Columbus to lead a large **fleet** across the Atlantic. Seventeen ships carried 1,500 people. Almost all of them had volunteered for the voyage.

The fleet left from Cádiz, Spain, on September 25, 1493. Once again, it stopped at the Canary Islands. On November 5, the ships arrived at islands south of the first voyage. Columbus added the Leeward Islands and Puerto Rico to the list of his discoveries.

The ships sailed farther and reached Hispaniola. The natives on the island had destroyed the first colony, and the Spanish colonists were missing.

King Ferdinand

1588
Drake helped England win the Battle of Gravelines against Spain's Invincible Armada

1581
Drake knighted by Queen Elizabeth I

1596
Drake died

The newly arrived colonists made another settlement, called Isabella. Columbus soon left for more exploring. After discovering Jamaica, he returned to Hispaniola. **Chaos** had taken over there.

Some colonists had taken over one of the ships and returned to Spain. There, they complained to Ferdinand and Isabella about the state of the new settlement. In 1496, Columbus put his brother Bartholomew in charge of the colony. He returned to Spain to defend himself.

Queen Isabella

A Third Voyage

Because he was a good speaker, Columbus was able to clear his name with the king and queen. They allowed him to keep his titles. They even granted him a third voyage to the new colony.

Columbus wasn't as successful with the commoners, however. Rumors had spread about the terrible conditions on Hispaniola. And the voyages were not profitable, as the colonists had hoped. So, the excitement of the New World was wearing off.

For his third voyage, Columbus was unable to get enough crew members for six ships. Ferdinand and Isabella had to pardon prisoners. They were then forced to man the **fleet**.

On May 30, 1498, Columbus set sail from Sanlúcar de Barrameda, Spain. This time, he took an even more southerly course. Ferdinand and Isabella had heard of land south of the islands that Columbus had already been to.

The king and queen wanted him to claim it for Spain.

Two months later, the new course landed the crew on the island of Trinidad. Next, they sailed across the Gulf of Paria to the coast of Venezuela.

At the Venezuela landing, Columbus noticed the mouth of a river. Freshwater poured from it into the sea. From this observation, he knew that this land could not be an island.

Christopher Columbus

1778
Cook became the first European to record Hawaiian Islands; Boone captured by Shawnee

1775
Boone cut the Wilderness Road from Virginia to Kentucky

1779
Cook died

But Columbus doubted this land was the Asian continent. In fact, a year earlier Columbus had heard of a discovery. Nova Scotia and Newfoundland had been found by John Cabot. This meant there was land between Europe and Asia.

Now Columbus had more doubts about his previous discoveries. But, he did not say anything about his doubts. He made notes in his journal, and then headed back to Hispaniola.

Isabella and Ferdinand had been told of the worsening conditions in Hispaniola. So in 1500, a new governor was sent to Columbus's colony. Columbus was then arrested and sent back to Spain in chains.

When he got to Spain, Columbus was immediately released. But his reputation had been destroyed. By this time, other explorers such as Amerigo Vespucci had discovered much of the northeast coast of South America. This was the continent Columbus had noted in his journal.

1813
John C. Frémont born

1842
Frémont's first independent surveying mission

1820
Boone died

Would you let Columbus lead another expedition? What would be the reasons for your decision?

Throughout the voyage to Spain, Columbus refused to remove his chains.

The High Voyage

Columbus still hoped to find a passage to Asia. He called his fourth expedition the High Voyage. This was his last chance to prove his theory. On this fourth expedition, Columbus hoped to sail farther west. If he could sail just beyond the islands, he might finally reach Asia.

On May 9, 1502, a **fleet** of four ships left Cádiz, Spain. Among Columbus's crew was his youngest son, Fernando. After surviving a **hurricane**, the fleet reached Central America.

The fleet landed on the shores of Honduras at the end of July. The ships continued in **dangerous** waters to the south. Columbus landed again and attempted to found a settlement. But, he abandoned it when one of his ships was lost in an attack by natives.

Captain Columbus became sick with **malaria** and decided to head back to Hispaniola. On the way, bad

1856
Frémont ran for president of the United States but lost

1845-1846
Frémont explored the Great Basin and the Pacific Coast, and fought in the Mexican War

1890
Frémont died

weather destroyed a ship. Soon, the two remaining ships had to be beached. They were damaged beyond repair. Columbus and his crew were **marooned** on Jamaica for one year.

Columbus was stranded on a beach on the island of Jamaica, much like this one.

1910
Jacques Cousteau born

1951
Cousteau's first expedition in the Red Sea

1942
Cousteau and Gagnan developed the Aqua-Lung for diving

Final Days

Columbus and 100 surviving crew members were rescued at the end of June 1504. They returned to Sanlúcar de Barrameda, Spain, on November 7, 1504. Columbus abandoned his hopes of finding a western route to Asia.

Queen Isabella, Columbus's biggest fan, died shortly after his return to Spain. With Isabella gone, Columbus's support also vanished. King Ferdinand listened to, but refused Columbus's requests for rewards for his discoveries.

Columbus moved to Valladolid, Spain. Christopher Columbus died there on May 21, 1506. He was 55 years old.

Columbus was not the first European to sail to the New World. It is believed Leif Eriksson and the Vikings landed on North America in the 1000s. However, Columbus's explorations marked the beginning of continuous European efforts to explore and colonize the Americas.

There are many statues of Columbus around the world. This statue is in Barcelona, Spain.

Glossary

caravan - a group of people traveling together for safety through difficult or dangerous country.

caravel - a type of small, fast sailing ship used by Columbus and other early navigators, with a broad bow and high stern.

chaos - a state of total confusion.

dangerous - able or likely to cause injury or harm.

era - a period of time or history.

fleet - a group of ships under one command.

gatekeeper - a person appointed to take toll money from people entering or leaving a city.

hurricane - a tropical storm with strong, circular winds, rain, thunder, and lightning.

hydrography - the mapping of bodies of water.

malaria - a disease spread by certain mosquitoes that causes chills and fever.

marooned - stuck on a deserted land without hope of escape.

rebel - to disobey an authority or the government.

uncharted - something that is unknown and, therefore, has not been recorded on a map, chart, or plan.

viceroy - a governor who acts as the representative of a king or queen.

Saying It

Amerigo Vespucci - ahm-ay-REE-goh vay-SPOOT-chee

Cádiz - KAH-theeth

Madeira - mah-DAYR-uh

Palos - PAH-lohs

Puerto Rico - PWEHR-toh REE-koh

Sanlúcar de Barrameda - sahn-LOO-kahr thay bah-rah-MAY-thah

Valladolid - bahl-yah-thoh-LEETH

Venezuela - veh-nuh-ZWAY-luh

Web Sites

To learn more about Christopher Columbus, visit ABDO Publishing Company on the World Wide Web at **www.abdopub.com**. Web sites about Christopher Columbus are featured on our Book Links page. These links are routinely monitored and updated to provide the most current information available.

Jacques Cousteau   *Sir Francis Drake*   *Vasco da Gama*

Hernán Cortés   *Hernando de Soto*   *John C. Frémont*

Index

A
Africa 10, 12
Asia 4, 5, 12, 16, 24, 26, 28
Atlantic Ocean 8, 9, 12, 20

B
Bahamas 16
British Isles 8

C
Cabot, John 24
Cádiz, Spain 20, 26
Canary Islands 12, 14, 20
Central America 26
China 16
Chios 7
Cuba 16

D
Dominican Republic 16

E
education 6, 8, 10
Enterprise of the Indies 12
Europe 4, 24, 28

F
family 6, 8, 10, 21, 26
Ferdinand (king of Spain) 13,
    17, 20, 21, 22, 23, 24, 28

G
Genoa, Italy 6, 7

H
Haiti 16
Hispaniola 16, 20, 21, 22, 24, 26
Honduras 26

I
Isabella (colony) 21
Isabella (queen of Spain) 13, 17,
    20, 21, 22, 23, 24, 28

J
Jamaica 21, 27
Japan 12, 16
John II (king of Portugal) 12

L
Leeward Islands 20
Leif Eriksson 28
Lisbon, Portugal 8, 10

M
Madeira 10
Mediterranean Sea 4, 7

N
Newfoundland 24
Niña 14, 16

**North America 12, 28
Nova Scotia 24**

O
Ottoman Empire 4

P
Palos, Spain 14
Paria, Gulf of 23
Pinta 14
Porto Santo 10
Portugal 8, 10, 12
Puerto Rico 20

S
San Salvador 16
Sanlúcar de Barrameda, Spain
    22, 28
Santa María 14, 16
South America 12, 24, 28
Spain 13, 16, 17, 21, 23, 24, 28

T
Trinidad 23
Turkey 7

V
Valladolid, Spain 28
Venezuela 23
Vespucci, Amerigo 24
Vikings 28